TRAIL NAME

LOCATION

DATE

COMPANIONS

START TIME

END TIME

DURATION

DISTANCE

ALTITUDE

TERRAIN LEVEL

EASY ○ 1 ○ 2 ○ 3 ○ 4 ○ 5 HARD

TRAIL TYPE

| ☐ LOOP | ☐ ONE WAY |
| ☐ OUT & BACK | ☐ OTHERS |

GEAR & EQUIPMENT

ANIMALS & PLANTS

ROUTE HIGHLIGHTS

MILESTONE	TIME	NOTE

TRAIL NAME

LOCATION

DATE

COMPANIONS

START TIME

END TIME

DURATION

DISTANCE

ALTITUDE

WEATHER CONDITIONS

TERRAIN LEVEL

EASY 1 2 3 4 5 HARD

TRAIL TYPE

| ☐ LOOP | ☐ ONE WAY |
| ☐ OUT & BACK | ☐ OTHERS |

GEAR & EQUIPMENT

ANIMALS & PLANTS

ROUTE HIGHLIGHTS

MILESTONE	TIME	NOTE

TRAIL NAME

LOCATION

DATE

COMPANIONS

START TIME

END TIME

DURATION

DISTANCE

ALTITUDE

WEATHER CONDITIONS

TERRAIN LEVEL

EASY 1 2 3 4 5 HARD

TRAIL TYPE

| ☐ LOOP | ☐ ONE WAY |
| ☐ OUT & BACK | ☐ OTHERS |

GEAR & EQUIPMENT

ANIMALS & PLANTS

ROUTE HIGHLIGHTS

MILESTONE	TIME	NOTE

TRAIL NAME

LOCATION

DATE

COMPANIONS

START TIME

END TIME

DURATION

DISTANCE

ALTITUDE

WEATHER CONDITIONS

TERRAIN LEVEL

EASY 1 2 3 4 5 HARD

TRAIL TYPE

- ☐ LOOP
- ☐ ONE WAY
- ☐ OUT & BACK
- ☐ OTHERS

GEAR & EQUIPMENT

ANIMALS & PLANTS

ROUTE HIGHLIGHTS

MILESTONE	TIME	NOTE

TRAIL NAME

LOCATION

DATE

COMPANIONS

START TIME

END TIME

DURATION

DISTANCE

ALTITUDE

WEATHER CONDITIONS

TERRAIN LEVEL

EASY 1 2 3 4 5 HARD

TRAIL TYPE

- [ ] LOOP
- [ ] ONE WAY
- [ ] OUT & BACK
- [ ] OTHERS

GEAR & EQUIPMENT

ANIMALS & PLANTS

ROUTE HIGHLIGHTS

MILESTONE	TIME	NOTE

TRAIL NAME

LOCATION

DATE

COMPANIONS

START TIME

END TIME

DURATION

DISTANCE

ALTITUDE

WEATHER CONDITIONS

TERRAIN LEVEL

EASY 1 2 3 4 5 HARD

TRAIL TYPE

| ☐ LOOP | ☐ ONE WAY |
| ☐ OUT & BACK | ☐ OTHERS |

GEAR & EQUIPMENT

ANIMALS & PLANTS

ROUTE HIGHLIGHTS

MILESTONE	TIME	NOTE

TRAIL NAME

LOCATION

DATE

COMPANIONS

START TIME

END TIME

DURATION

DISTANCE

ALTITUDE

WEATHER CONDITIONS

		☀	⛅	🌧	⛈	❄
	—	☐	☐	☐	☐	☐

TERRAIN LEVEL

	1	2	3	4	5	
EASY	○	○	○	○	○	HARD

TRAIL TYPE

☐ LOOP	☐ ONE WAY
☐ OUT & BACK	☐ OTHERS

GEAR & EQUIPMENT

ANIMALS & PLANTS

ROUTE HIGHLIGHTS

MILESTONE	TIME	NOTE

TRAIL NAME

LOCATION

DATE

COMPANIONS

START TIME

END TIME

DURATION

DISTANCE

ALTITUDE

WEATHER CONDITIONS

TERRAIN LEVEL

EASY 1 2 3 4 5 HARD

TRAIL TYPE

- ☐ LOOP
- ☐ ONE WAY
- ☐ OUT & BACK
- ☐ OTHERS

GEAR & EQUIPMENT

ANIMALS & PLANTS

ROUTE HIGHLIGHTS

MILESTONE	TIME	NOTE

TRAIL NAME

LOCATION

DATE

COMPANIONS

START TIME

END TIME

DURATION

DISTANCE

ALTITUDE

WEATHER CONDITIONS

TERRAIN LEVEL

EASY 1 2 3 4 5 HARD

TRAIL TYPE

| ☐ LOOP | ☐ ONE WAY |
| ☐ OUT & BACK | ☐ OTHERS |

GEAR & EQUIPMENT

ANIMALS & PLANTS

ROUTE HIGHLIGHTS

MILESTONE	TIME	NOTE

TRAIL NAME

LOCATION

DATE

COMPANIONS

START TIME

END TIME

DURATION

DISTANCE

ALTITUDE

WEATHER CONDITIONS

TERRAIN LEVEL

EASY 1 2 3 4 5 HARD

TRAIL TYPE

| ☐ LOOP | ☐ ONE WAY |
| ☐ OUT & BACK | ☐ OTHERS |

GEAR & EQUIPMENT

ANIMALS & PLANTS

ROUTE HIGHLIGHTS

MILESTONE	TIME	NOTE

TRAIL NAME

LOCATION

DATE

COMPANIONS

START TIME

END TIME

DURATION

DISTANCE

ALTITUDE

WEATHER CONDITIONS

TERRAIN LEVEL

EASY 1 2 3 4 5 HARD

TRAIL TYPE

- [ ] LOOP
- [ ] ONE WAY
- [ ] OUT & BACK
- [ ] OTHERS

GEAR & EQUIPMENT

ANIMALS & PLANTS

ROUTE HIGHLIGHTS

MILESTONE	TIME	NOTE

TRAIL NAME

LOCATION

DATE

COMPANIONS

START TIME

END TIME

DURATION

DISTANCE

ALTITUDE

WEATHER CONDITIONS

☐ ☐ ☐ ☐ ☐

TERRAIN LEVEL

EASY 1 2 3 4 5 HARD

TRAIL TYPE

☐ LOOP   ☐ ONE WAY

☐ OUT & BACK   ☐ OTHERS

GEAR & EQUIPMENT

ANIMALS & PLANTS

ROUTE HIGHLIGHTS

MILESTONE	TIME	NOTE

TRAIL NAME

LOCATION

DATE

COMPANIONS

START TIME

END TIME

DURATION

DISTANCE

ALTITUDE

WEATHER CONDITIONS

TERRAIN LEVEL

EASY 1 2 3 4 5 HARD

TRAIL TYPE

| ☐ LOOP | ☐ ONE WAY |
| ☐ OUT & BACK | ☐ OTHERS |

GEAR & EQUIPMENT

ANIMALS & PLANTS

ROUTE HIGHLIGHTS

MILESTONE	TIME	NOTE

TRAIL NAME	
LOCATION	
DATE	
COMPANIONS	

WEATHER CONDITIONS

	___	☀	⛅	☁	🌧	❄
	___	☐	☐	☐	☐	☐

START TIME	
END TIME	
DURATION	
DISTANCE	
ALTITUDE	

TERRAIN LEVEL

EASY 1 2 3 4 5 HARD
○ ○ ○ ○ ○

TRAIL TYPE

☐ LOOP	☐ ONE WAY
☐ OUT & BACK	☐ OTHERS

GEAR & EQUIPMENT

ANIMALS & PLANTS

ROUTE HIGHLIGHTS

MILESTONE	TIME	NOTE

TRAIL NAME

LOCATION

DATE

COMPANIONS

START TIME

END TIME

DURATION

DISTANCE

ALTITUDE

WEATHER CONDITIONS

TERRAIN LEVEL

EASY	1	2	3	4	5	HARD
○	○	○	○	○		

TRAIL TYPE

☐ LOOP	☐ ONE WAY
☐ OUT & BACK	☐ OTHERS

GEAR & EQUIPMENT

ANIMALS & PLANTS

ROUTE HIGHLIGHTS

MILESTONE	TIME	NOTE

TRAIL NAME

LOCATION

DATE

COMPANIONS

START TIME

END TIME

DURATION

DISTANCE

ALTITUDE

WEATHER CONDITIONS

TERRAIN LEVEL

EASY 1 2 3 4 5 HARD

TRAIL TYPE

☐ LOOP	☐ ONE WAY
☐ OUT & BACK	☐ OTHERS

GEAR & EQUIPMENT

ANIMALS & PLANTS

ROUTE HIGHLIGHTS

MILESTONE	TIME	NOTE

TRAIL NAME

LOCATION

DATE

COMPANIONS

START TIME

END TIME

DURATION

DISTANCE

ALTITUDE

WEATHER CONDITIONS

TERRAIN LEVEL

EASY 1 2 3 4 5 HARD

TRAIL TYPE

- [ ] LOOP
- [ ] ONE WAY
- [ ] OUT & BACK
- [ ] OTHERS

GEAR & EQUIPMENT

ANIMALS & PLANTS

ROUTE HIGHLIGHTS

MILESTONE	TIME	NOTE

TRAIL NAME

LOCATION

DATE

COMPANIONS

START TIME

END TIME

DURATION

DISTANCE

ALTITUDE

WEATHER CONDITIONS

☀ ⛅ ☁ 🌧 ❄
☐ ☐ ☐ ☐ ☐

TERRAIN LEVEL

EASY 1 ○ 2 ○ 3 ○ 4 ○ 5 ○ HARD

TRAIL TYPE

| ☐ LOOP | ☐ ONE WAY |
| ☐ OUT & BACK | ☐ OTHERS |

GEAR & EQUIPMENT

ANIMALS & PLANTS

ROUTE HIGHLIGHTS

MILESTONE	TIME	NOTE

TRAIL NAME

LOCATION

DATE

COMPANIONS

START TIME

END TIME

DURATION

DISTANCE

ALTITUDE

WEATHER CONDITIONS

TERRAIN LEVEL

EASY 1 2 3 4 5 HARD

TRAIL TYPE

| ☐ LOOP | ☐ ONE WAY |
| ☐ OUT & BACK | ☐ OTHERS |

GEAR & EQUIPMENT

ANIMALS & PLANTS

ROUTE HIGHLIGHTS

MILESTONE	TIME	NOTE

TRAIL NAME

LOCATION

DATE

COMPANIONS

START TIME

END TIME

DURATION

DISTANCE

ALTITUDE

WEATHER CONDITIONS

TERRAIN LEVEL

	1	2	3	4	5	
EASY	○	○	○	○	○	HARD

TRAIL TYPE

☐ LOOP   ☐ ONE WAY

☐ OUT & BACK   ☐ OTHERS

GEAR & EQUIPMENT

ANIMALS & PLANTS

ROUTE HIGHLIGHTS

MILESTONE	TIME	NOTE

TRAIL NAME

LOCATION

DATE

COMPANIONS

START TIME

END TIME

DURATION

DISTANCE

ALTITUDE

WEATHER CONDITIONS

🌡 —— ☀ ⛅ 🌧 ⛈ ❄

🚩 —— ☐ ☐ ☐ ☐ ☐

TERRAIN LEVEL

EASY ○ 1 ○ 2 ○ 3 ○ 4 ○ 5 HARD

TRAIL TYPE

| ☐ LOOP | ☐ ONE WAY |
| ☐ OUT & BACK | ☐ OTHERS |

GEAR & EQUIPMENT

ANIMALS & PLANTS

ROUTE HIGHLIGHTS

MILESTONE	TIME	NOTE

TRAIL NAME	
LOCATION	
DATE	
COMPANIONS	

WEATHER CONDITIONS

Temperature — ☀ ⛅ 🌧 ⛈ ❄

Wind — ☐ ☐ ☐ ☐ ☐

START TIME	
END TIME	
DURATION	
DISTANCE	
ALTITUDE	

TERRAIN LEVEL

EASY 1 2 3 4 5 HARD

TRAIL TYPE

☐ LOOP	☐ ONE WAY
☐ OUT & BACK	☐ OTHERS

GEAR & EQUIPMENT

ANIMALS & PLANTS

ROUTE HIGHLIGHTS

MILESTONE	TIME	NOTE

TRAIL NAME

LOCATION

DATE

COMPANIONS

START TIME

END TIME

DURATION

DISTANCE

ALTITUDE

WEATHER CONDITIONS

TERRAIN LEVEL

1   2   3   4   5

EASY   HARD

TRAIL TYPE

- [ ] LOOP
- [ ] ONE WAY
- [ ] OUT & BACK
- [ ] OTHERS

GEAR & EQUIPMENT

ANIMALS & PLANTS

ROUTE HIGHLIGHTS

MILESTONE	TIME	NOTE

TRAIL NAME

LOCATION

DATE

COMPANIONS

START TIME

END TIME

DURATION

DISTANCE

ALTITUDE

WEATHER CONDITIONS

TERRAIN LEVEL

EASY 1   2   3   4   5 HARD

TRAIL TYPE

| ☐ LOOP | ☐ ONE WAY |
| ☐ OUT & BACK | ☐ OTHERS |

GEAR & EQUIPMENT

ANIMALS & PLANTS

ROUTE HIGHLIGHTS

MILESTONE	TIME	NOTE

TRAIL NAME

LOCATION

DATE

COMPANIONS

START TIME

END TIME

DURATION

DISTANCE

ALTITUDE

WEATHER CONDITIONS

TERRAIN LEVEL

	1	2	3	4	5	
EASY	○	○	○	○	○	HARD

TRAIL TYPE

☐ LOOP ☐ ONE WAY

☐ OUT & BACK ☐ OTHERS

GEAR & EQUIPMENT

ANIMALS & PLANTS

ROUTE HIGHLIGHTS

MILESTONE	TIME	NOTE

TRAIL NAME

LOCATION

DATE

COMPANIONS

START TIME

END TIME

DURATION

DISTANCE

ALTITUDE

WEATHER CONDITIONS

TERRAIN LEVEL

| EASY | 1 | 2 | 3 | 4 | 5 | HARD |

TRAIL TYPE

| ☐ LOOP | ☐ ONE WAY |
| ☐ OUT & BACK | ☐ OTHERS |

GEAR & EQUIPMENT

ANIMALS & PLANTS

ROUTE HIGHLIGHTS

MILESTONE	TIME	NOTE

TRAIL NAME

LOCATION

DATE

COMPANIONS

START TIME

END TIME

DURATION

DISTANCE

ALTITUDE

WEATHER CONDITIONS

🌡 —	☀	⛅	🌧	⛈	❄
🚩 —	☐	☐	☐	☐	☐

TERRAIN LEVEL

EASY 1 2 3 4 5 HARD

TRAIL TYPE

☐ LOOP	☐ ONE WAY
☐ OUT & BACK	☐ OTHERS

GEAR & EQUIPMENT

ANIMALS & PLANTS

ROUTE HIGHLIGHTS

MILESTONE	TIME	NOTE

TRAIL NAME

LOCATION

DATE

COMPANIONS

START TIME

END TIME

DURATION

DISTANCE

ALTITUDE

WEATHER CONDITIONS

TERRAIN LEVEL

EASY 1 2 3 4 5 HARD

TRAIL TYPE

- [ ] LOOP
- [ ] ONE WAY
- [ ] OUT & BACK
- [ ] OTHERS

GEAR & EQUIPMENT

ANIMALS & PLANTS

ROUTE HIGHLIGHTS

MILESTONE	TIME	NOTE

TRAIL NAME

LOCATION

DATE

COMPANIONS

START TIME

END TIME

DURATION

DISTANCE

ALTITUDE

WEATHER CONDITIONS

☀ ⛅ ☁ 🌧 ❄

☐ ☐ ☐ ☐ ☐

TERRAIN LEVEL

EASY 1 ○ 2 ○ 3 ○ 4 ○ 5 HARD

TRAIL TYPE

| ☐ LOOP | ☐ ONE WAY |
| ☐ OUT & BACK | ☐ OTHERS |

GEAR & EQUIPMENT

ANIMALS & PLANTS

ROUTE HIGHLIGHTS

MILESTONE	TIME	NOTE

TRAIL NAME

LOCATION

DATE

COMPANIONS

START TIME

END TIME

DURATION

DISTANCE

ALTITUDE

WEATHER CONDITIONS

☐ ☐ ☐ ☐ ☐

TERRAIN LEVEL

EASY 1 2 3 4 5 HARD

TRAIL TYPE

☐ LOOP   ☐ ONE WAY

☐ OUT & BACK   ☐ OTHERS

GEAR & EQUIPMENT

ANIMALS & PLANTS

ROUTE HIGHLIGHTS

MILESTONE	TIME	NOTE

TRAIL NAME

LOCATION

DATE

COMPANIONS

START TIME

END TIME

DURATION

DISTANCE

ALTITUDE

WEATHER CONDITIONS

TERRAIN LEVEL

EASY 1 2 3 4 5 HARD

TRAIL TYPE

- [ ] LOOP
- [ ] ONE WAY
- [ ] OUT & BACK
- [ ] OTHERS

GEAR & EQUIPMENT

ANIMALS & PLANTS

ROUTE HIGHLIGHTS

MILESTONE	TIME	NOTE

TRAIL NAME

LOCATION

DATE

COMPANIONS

START TIME

END TIME

DURATION

DISTANCE

ALTITUDE

WEATHER CONDITIONS

TERRAIN LEVEL

	1	2	3	4	5	
EASY	○	○	○	○	○	HARD

TRAIL TYPE

☐ LOOP	☐ ONE WAY
☐ OUT & BACK	☐ OTHERS

GEAR & EQUIPMENT

ANIMALS & PLANTS

ROUTE HIGHLIGHTS

MILESTONE	TIME	NOTE

TRAIL NAME

LOCATION

DATE

COMPANIONS

START TIME

END TIME

DURATION

DISTANCE

ALTITUDE

WEATHER CONDITIONS

TERRAIN LEVEL

| EASY | 1 | 2 | 3 | 4 | 5 | HARD |

TRAIL TYPE

| ☐ LOOP | ☐ ONE WAY |
| ☐ OUT & BACK | ☐ OTHERS |

GEAR & EQUIPMENT

ANIMALS & PLANTS

ROUTE HIGHLIGHTS

MILESTONE	TIME	NOTE

TRAIL NAME

LOCATION

DATE

COMPANIONS

START TIME

END TIME

DURATION

DISTANCE

ALTITUDE

WEATHER CONDITIONS

TERRAIN LEVEL

EASY 1 2 3 4 5 HARD

TRAIL TYPE

- [ ] LOOP
- [ ] ONE WAY
- [ ] OUT & BACK
- [ ] OTHERS

GEAR & EQUIPMENT

ANIMALS & PLANTS

ROUTE HIGHLIGHTS

MILESTONE	TIME	NOTE

TRAIL NAME

LOCATION

DATE

COMPANIONS

START TIME

END TIME

DURATION

DISTANCE

ALTITUDE

WEATHER CONDITIONS

TERRAIN LEVEL

EASY 1 2 3 4 5 HARD

TRAIL TYPE

☐ LOOP	☐ ONE WAY
☐ OUT & BACK	☐ OTHERS

GEAR & EQUIPMENT

ANIMALS & PLANTS

ROUTE HIGHLIGHTS

MILESTONE	TIME	NOTE

TRAIL NAME

LOCATION

DATE

COMPANIONS

START TIME

END TIME

DURATION

DISTANCE

ALTITUDE

WEATHER CONDITIONS

TERRAIN LEVEL

EASY 1   2   3   4   5 HARD

TRAIL TYPE

- [ ] LOOP
- [ ] ONE WAY
- [ ] OUT & BACK
- [ ] OTHERS

GEAR & EQUIPMENT

ANIMALS & PLANTS

ROUTE HIGHLIGHTS

MILESTONE	TIME	NOTE

TRAIL NAME

LOCATION

DATE

COMPANIONS

START TIME

END TIME

DURATION

DISTANCE

ALTITUDE

WEATHER CONDITIONS

TERRAIN LEVEL

EASY 1 2 3 4 5 HARD

TRAIL TYPE

☐ LOOP		☐ ONE WAY	
☐ OUT & BACK		☐ OTHERS	

GEAR & EQUIPMENT

ANIMALS & PLANTS

ROUTE HIGHLIGHTS

MILESTONE	TIME	NOTE

TRAIL NAME

LOCATION

DATE

COMPANIONS

START TIME

END TIME

DURATION

DISTANCE

ALTITUDE

WEATHER CONDITIONS

TERRAIN LEVEL

	1	2	3	4	5	
EASY	◯	◯	◯	◯	◯	HARD

TRAIL TYPE

☐ LOOP	☐ ONE WAY
☐ OUT & BACK	☐ OTHERS

GEAR & EQUIPMENT

ANIMALS & PLANTS

ROUTE HIGHLIGHTS

MILESTONE	TIME	NOTE

TRAIL NAME

LOCATION

DATE

COMPANIONS

START TIME

END TIME

DURATION

DISTANCE

ALTITUDE

WEATHER CONDITIONS

TERRAIN LEVEL

EASY	1	2	3	4	5	HARD

TRAIL TYPE

☐ LOOP	☐ ONE WAY
☐ OUT & BACK	☐ OTHERS

GEAR & EQUIPMENT

ANIMALS & PLANTS

ROUTE HIGHLIGHTS

MILESTONE	TIME	NOTE

TRAIL NAME

LOCATION

DATE

COMPANIONS

START TIME

END TIME

DURATION

DISTANCE

ALTITUDE

WEATHER CONDITIONS

TERRAIN LEVEL

1   2   3   4   5

EASY   ○   ○   ○   ○   ○   HARD

TRAIL TYPE

- ☐ LOOP
- ☐ ONE WAY
- ☐ OUT & BACK
- ☐ OTHERS

GEAR & EQUIPMENT

ANIMALS & PLANTS

ROUTE HIGHLIGHTS

MILESTONE	TIME	NOTE

TRAIL NAME
LOCATION
DATE
COMPANIONS

START TIME
END TIME
DURATION
DISTANCE
ALTITUDE

WEATHER CONDITIONS

TERRAIN LEVEL

EASY 1 2 3 4 5 HARD

TRAIL TYPE

☐ LOOP	☐ ONE WAY
☐ OUT & BACK	☐ OTHERS

GEAR & EQUIPMENT

ANIMALS & PLANTS

ROUTE HIGHLIGHTS

MILESTONE	TIME	NOTE

TRAIL NAME

LOCATION

DATE

COMPANIONS

START TIME

END TIME

DURATION

DISTANCE

ALTITUDE

WEATHER CONDITIONS

TERRAIN LEVEL

EASY 1 2 3 4 5 HARD

TRAIL TYPE

☐ LOOP | ☐ ONE WAY
☐ OUT & BACK | ☐ OTHERS

GEAR & EQUIPMENT

ANIMALS & PLANTS

ROUTE HIGHLIGHTS

MILESTONE	TIME	NOTE

TRAIL NAME

LOCATION

DATE

COMPANIONS

START TIME

END TIME

DURATION

DISTANCE

ALTITUDE

WEATHER CONDITIONS

TERRAIN LEVEL

EASY 1 2 3 4 5 HARD

TRAIL TYPE

| ☐ LOOP | ☐ ONE WAY |
| ☐ OUT & BACK | ☐ OTHERS |

GEAR & EQUIPMENT

ANIMALS & PLANTS

ROUTE HIGHLIGHTS

MILESTONE	TIME	NOTE

TRAIL NAME

LOCATION

DATE

COMPANIONS

START TIME

END TIME

DURATION

DISTANCE

ALTITUDE

WEATHER CONDITIONS

TERRAIN LEVEL

EASY 1 2 3 4 5 HARD

TRAIL TYPE

| ☐ LOOP | ☐ ONE WAY |
| ☐ OUT & BACK | ☐ OTHERS |

GEAR & EQUIPMENT

ANIMALS & PLANTS

ROUTE HIGHLIGHTS

MILESTONE	TIME	NOTE

TRAIL NAME

LOCATION

DATE

COMPANIONS

START TIME

END TIME

DURATION

DISTANCE

ALTITUDE

WEATHER CONDITIONS

TERRAIN LEVEL

	1	2	3	4	5	
EASY	○	○	○	○	○	HARD

TRAIL TYPE

☐ LOOP	☐ ONE WAY
☐ OUT & BACK	☐ OTHERS

GEAR & EQUIPMENT

ANIMALS & PLANTS

ROUTE HIGHLIGHTS

MILESTONE	TIME	NOTE

TRAIL NAME

LOCATION

DATE

COMPANIONS

START TIME

END TIME

DURATION

DISTANCE

ALTITUDE

WEATHER CONDITIONS

TERRAIN LEVEL

EASY 1 2 3 4 5 HARD

TRAIL TYPE

☐ LOOP   ☐ ONE WAY

☐ OUT & BACK   ☐ OTHERS

GEAR & EQUIPMENT

ANIMALS & PLANTS

ROUTE HIGHLIGHTS

MILESTONE	TIME	NOTE

	TRAIL NAME
	LOCATION
	DATE
	COMPANIONS

	START TIME
	END TIME
	DURATION
	DISTANCE
	ALTITUDE

WEATHER CONDITIONS

		☀	⛅	🌧	⛈	❄
	—	☐	☐	☐	☐	☐

TERRAIN LEVEL

	1	2	3	4	5	
EASY	○	○	○	○	○	HARD

TRAIL TYPE

☐ LOOP	☐ ONE WAY
☐ OUT & BACK	☐ OTHERS

GEAR & EQUIPMENT

ANIMALS & PLANTS

ROUTE HIGHLIGHTS

MILESTONE	TIME	NOTE

TRAIL NAME

LOCATION

DATE

COMPANIONS

START TIME

END TIME

DURATION

DISTANCE

ALTITUDE

WEATHER CONDITIONS

🌡 _____ ☀ ⛅ 🌧 ⛈ ❄

🎏 _____ ☐ ☐ ☐ ☐ ☐

TERRAIN LEVEL

EASY ○ 1 ○ 2 ○ 3 ○ 4 ○ 5 HARD

TRAIL TYPE

| ☐ LOOP | ☐ ONE WAY |
| ☐ OUT & BACK | ☐ OTHERS |

GEAR & EQUIPMENT

ANIMALS & PLANTS

ROUTE HIGHLIGHTS

MILESTONE	TIME	NOTE

TRAIL NAME

LOCATION

DATE

COMPANIONS

START TIME

END TIME

DURATION

DISTANCE

ALTITUDE

WEATHER CONDITIONS

TERRAIN LEVEL

	1	2	3	4	5	
EASY	○	○	○	○	○	HARD

TRAIL TYPE

☐ LOOP	☐ ONE WAY
☐ OUT & BACK	☐ OTHERS

GEAR & EQUIPMENT

ANIMALS & PLANTS

ROUTE HIGHLIGHTS

MILESTONE	TIME	NOTE

TRAIL NAME

LOCATION

DATE

COMPANIONS

START TIME

END TIME

DURATION

DISTANCE

ALTITUDE

WEATHER CONDITIONS

TERRAIN LEVEL

EASY 1 2 3 4 5 HARD

TRAIL TYPE

LOOP	ONE WAY
OUT & BACK	OTHERS

GEAR & EQUIPMENT

ANIMALS & PLANTS

ROUTE HIGHLIGHTS

MILESTONE	TIME	NOTE

TRAIL NAME

LOCATION

DATE

COMPANIONS

START TIME

END TIME

DURATION

DISTANCE

ALTITUDE

WEATHER CONDITIONS

TERRAIN LEVEL

EASY 1 2 3 4 5 HARD

TRAIL TYPE

- [ ] LOOP
- [ ] ONE WAY
- [ ] OUT & BACK
- [ ] OTHERS

GEAR & EQUIPMENT

ANIMALS & PLANTS

ROUTE HIGHLIGHTS

MILESTONE	TIME	NOTE

TRAIL NAME

LOCATION

DATE

COMPANIONS

START TIME

END TIME

DURATION

DISTANCE

ALTITUDE

WEATHER CONDITIONS

TERRAIN LEVEL

EASY 1 2 3 4 5 HARD

TRAIL TYPE

- [ ] LOOP
- [ ] ONE WAY
- [ ] OUT & BACK
- [ ] OTHERS

GEAR & EQUIPMENT

ANIMALS & PLANTS

ROUTE HIGHLIGHTS

MILESTONE	TIME	NOTE

TRAIL NAME

LOCATION

DATE

COMPANIONS

START TIME

END TIME

DURATION

DISTANCE

ALTITUDE

WEATHER CONDITIONS

TERRAIN LEVEL

EASY 1 2 3 4 5 HARD

TRAIL TYPE

| ☐ LOOP | ☐ ONE WAY |
| ☐ OUT & BACK | ☐ OTHERS |

GEAR & EQUIPMENT

ANIMALS & PLANTS

ROUTE HIGHLIGHTS

MILESTONE	TIME	NOTE

TRAIL NAME

LOCATION

DATE

COMPANIONS

START TIME

END TIME

DURATION

DISTANCE

ALTITUDE

WEATHER CONDITIONS

TERRAIN LEVEL

EASY 1 2 3 4 5 HARD

TRAIL TYPE

| ☐ LOOP | ☐ ONE WAY |
| ☐ OUT & BACK | ☐ OTHERS |

GEAR & EQUIPMENT

ANIMALS & PLANTS

ROUTE HIGHLIGHTS

MILESTONE	TIME	NOTE

TRAIL NAME

LOCATION

DATE

COMPANIONS

START TIME

END TIME

DURATION

DISTANCE

ALTITUDE

WEATHER CONDITIONS

☐	☐	☐	☐	☐

TERRAIN LEVEL

EASY ○ 1 ○ 2 ○ 3 ○ 4 ○ 5 HARD

TRAIL TYPE

☐ LOOP	☐ ONE WAY
☐ OUT & BACK	☐ OTHERS

GEAR & EQUIPMENT

ANIMALS & PLANTS

ROUTE HIGHLIGHTS

MILESTONE	TIME	NOTE

TRAIL NAME

LOCATION

DATE

COMPANIONS

START TIME

END TIME

DURATION

DISTANCE

ALTITUDE

WEATHER CONDITIONS

TERRAIN LEVEL

1   2   3   4   5

EASY   HARD

TRAIL TYPE

☐ LOOP   ☐ ONE WAY

☐ OUT & BACK   ☐ OTHERS

GEAR & EQUIPMENT

ANIMALS & PLANTS

ROUTE HIGHLIGHTS

MILESTONE	TIME	NOTE

TRAIL NAME

LOCATION

DATE

COMPANIONS

START TIME

END TIME

DURATION

DISTANCE

ALTITUDE

WEATHER CONDITIONS

TERRAIN LEVEL

EASY 1 2 3 4 5 HARD

TRAIL TYPE

☐ LOOP   ☐ ONE WAY

☐ OUT & BACK   ☐ OTHERS

GEAR & EQUIPMENT

ANIMALS & PLANTS

ROUTE HIGHLIGHTS

MILESTONE	TIME	NOTE

	TRAIL NAME
	LOCATION
	DATE
	COMPANIONS

	START TIME
	END TIME
	DURATION
	DISTANCE
	ALTITUDE

WEATHER CONDITIONS

TERRAIN LEVEL

EASY 1 2 3 4 5 HARD

TRAIL TYPE

	LOOP		ONE WAY
	OUT & BACK		OTHERS

GEAR & EQUIPMENT

ANIMALS & PLANTS

ROUTE HIGHLIGHTS

MILESTONE	TIME	NOTE

TRAIL NAME

LOCATION

DATE

COMPANIONS

START TIME

END TIME

DURATION

DISTANCE

ALTITUDE

WEATHER CONDITIONS

TERRAIN LEVEL

EASY 1 2 3 4 5 HARD

TRAIL TYPE

☐ LOOP ☐ ONE WAY

☐ OUT & BACK ☐ OTHERS

GEAR & EQUIPMENT

ANIMALS & PLANTS

ROUTE HIGHLIGHTS

MILESTONE	TIME	NOTE

TRAIL NAME

LOCATION

DATE

COMPANIONS

START TIME

END TIME

DURATION

DISTANCE

ALTITUDE

WEATHER CONDITIONS

🌡 ———   ☀ ⛅ 🌧 ⛈ ❄

🚩 ———   ☐ ☐ ☐ ☐ ☐

TERRAIN LEVEL

EASY 1 ○ 2 ○ 3 ○ 4 ○ 5 ○ HARD

TRAIL TYPE

| ☐ LOOP | ☐ ONE WAY |
| ☐ OUT & BACK | ☐ OTHERS |

GEAR & EQUIPMENT

ANIMALS & PLANTS

ROUTE HIGHLIGHTS

MILESTONE	TIME	NOTE

TRAIL NAME

LOCATION

DATE

COMPANIONS

START TIME

END TIME

DURATION

DISTANCE

ALTITUDE

WEATHER CONDITIONS

TERRAIN LEVEL

	1	2	3	4	5	
EASY	○	○	○	○	○	HARD

TRAIL TYPE

- [ ] LOOP
- [ ] ONE WAY
- [ ] OUT & BACK
- [ ] OTHERS

GEAR & EQUIPMENT

ANIMALS & PLANTS

ROUTE HIGHLIGHTS

MILESTONE	TIME	NOTE

TRAIL NAME

LOCATION

DATE

COMPANIONS

START TIME

END TIME

DURATION

DISTANCE

ALTITUDE

WEATHER CONDITIONS

TERRAIN LEVEL

EASY 1 2 3 4 5 HARD

TRAIL TYPE

- [ ] LOOP
- [ ] ONE WAY
- [ ] OUT & BACK
- [ ] OTHERS

GEAR & EQUIPMENT

ANIMALS & PLANTS

ROUTE HIGHLIGHTS

MILESTONE	TIME	NOTE

TRAIL NAME	
LOCATION	
DATE	
COMPANIONS	

WEATHER CONDITIONS

🌡 ____ ☀ ⛅ ☁ 🌧 ❄

🚩 ____ ☐ ☐ ☐ ☐ ☐

START TIME	
END TIME	
DURATION	
DISTANCE	
ALTITUDE	

TERRAIN LEVEL

EASY 1 2 3 4 5 HARD
○ ○ ○ ○ ○

TRAIL TYPE

☐ LOOP	☐ ONE WAY
☐ OUT & BACK	☐ OTHERS

GEAR & EQUIPMENT

ANIMALS & PLANTS

ROUTE HIGHLIGHTS

MILESTONE	TIME	NOTE

TRAIL NAME

LOCATION

DATE

COMPANIONS

START TIME

END TIME

DURATION

DISTANCE

ALTITUDE

WEATHER CONDITIONS

TERRAIN LEVEL

EASY 1 2 3 4 5 HARD

TRAIL TYPE

- [ ] LOOP
- [ ] ONE WAY
- [ ] OUT & BACK
- [ ] OTHERS

GEAR & EQUIPMENT

ANIMALS & PLANTS

ROUTE HIGHLIGHTS

MILESTONE	TIME	NOTE

TRAIL NAME

LOCATION

DATE

COMPANIONS

START TIME

END TIME

DURATION

DISTANCE

ALTITUDE

WEATHER CONDITIONS

TERRAIN LEVEL

EASY   1   2   3   4   5   HARD

TRAIL TYPE

| ☐ LOOP | ☐ ONE WAY |
| ☐ OUT & BACK | ☐ OTHERS |

GEAR & EQUIPMENT

ANIMALS & PLANTS

ROUTE HIGHLIGHTS

MILESTONE	TIME	NOTE

TRAIL NAME

LOCATION

DATE

COMPANIONS

START TIME

END TIME

DURATION

DISTANCE

ALTITUDE

WEATHER CONDITIONS

TERRAIN LEVEL

EASY   1   2   3   4   5   HARD

TRAIL TYPE

| ☐ LOOP | ☐ ONE WAY |
| ☐ OUT & BACK | ☐ OTHERS |

GEAR & EQUIPMENT

ANIMALS & PLANTS

ROUTE HIGHLIGHTS

MILESTONE	TIME	NOTE

TRAIL NAME

LOCATION

DATE

COMPANIONS

START TIME

END TIME

DURATION

DISTANCE

ALTITUDE

WEATHER CONDITIONS

TERRAIN LEVEL

EASY 1 2 3 4 5 HARD

TRAIL TYPE

☐ LOOP	☐ ONE WAY
☐ OUT & BACK	☐ OTHERS

GEAR & EQUIPMENT

ANIMALS & PLANTS

ROUTE HIGHLIGHTS

MILESTONE	TIME	NOTE

TRAIL NAME

LOCATION

DATE

COMPANIONS

START TIME

END TIME

DURATION

DISTANCE

ALTITUDE

WEATHER CONDITIONS

TERRAIN LEVEL

EASY 1 2 3 4 5 HARD

TRAIL TYPE

☐ LOOP ☐ ONE WAY

☐ OUT & BACK ☐ OTHERS

GEAR & EQUIPMENT

ANIMALS & PLANTS

ROUTE HIGHLIGHTS

MILESTONE	TIME	NOTE

TRAIL NAME

LOCATION

DATE

COMPANIONS

START TIME

END TIME

DURATION

DISTANCE

ALTITUDE

WEATHER CONDITIONS

TERRAIN LEVEL

| EASY | 1 | 2 | 3 | 4 | 5 | HARD |

TRAIL TYPE

| ☐ LOOP | ☐ ONE WAY |
| ☐ OUT & BACK | ☐ OTHERS |

GEAR & EQUIPMENT

ANIMALS & PLANTS

ROUTE HIGHLIGHTS

MILESTONE	TIME	NOTE

	TRAIL NAME
	LOCATION
	DATE
	COMPANIONS

	START TIME
	END TIME
	DURATION
	DISTANCE
	ALTITUDE

WEATHER CONDITIONS

TERRAIN LEVEL

EASY ○ 1 ○ 2 ○ 3 ○ 4 ○ 5 HARD

TRAIL TYPE

☐ LOOP	☐ ONE WAY
☐ OUT & BACK	☐ OTHERS

GEAR & EQUIPMENT

ANIMALS & PLANTS

ROUTE HIGHLIGHTS

MILESTONE	TIME	NOTE

TRAIL NAME

LOCATION

DATE

COMPANIONS

START TIME

END TIME

DURATION

DISTANCE

ALTITUDE

WEATHER CONDITIONS

TERRAIN LEVEL

	1	2	3	4	5	
EASY	○	○	○	○	○	HARD

TRAIL TYPE

☐ LOOP   ☐ ONE WAY

☐ OUT & BACK   ☐ OTHERS

GEAR & EQUIPMENT

ANIMALS & PLANTS

ROUTE HIGHLIGHTS

MILESTONE	TIME	NOTE

TRAIL NAME

LOCATION

DATE

COMPANIONS

START TIME

END TIME

DURATION

DISTANCE

ALTITUDE

WEATHER CONDITIONS

TERRAIN LEVEL

EASY 1   2   3   4   5 HARD

TRAIL TYPE

| ☐ LOOP | ☐ ONE WAY |
| ☐ OUT & BACK | ☐ OTHERS |

GEAR & EQUIPMENT

ANIMALS & PLANTS

ROUTE HIGHLIGHTS

MILESTONE	TIME	NOTE

TRAIL NAME

LOCATION

DATE

COMPANIONS

START TIME

END TIME

DURATION

DISTANCE

ALTITUDE

WEATHER CONDITIONS

TERRAIN LEVEL

	1	2	3	4	5	
EASY	○	○	○	○	○	HARD

TRAIL TYPE

- [ ] LOOP
- [ ] ONE WAY
- [ ] OUT & BACK
- [ ] OTHERS

GEAR & EQUIPMENT

ANIMALS & PLANTS

ROUTE HIGHLIGHTS

MILESTONE	TIME	NOTE

TRAIL NAME

LOCATION

DATE

COMPANIONS

START TIME

END TIME

DURATION

DISTANCE

ALTITUDE

WEATHER CONDITIONS

TERRAIN LEVEL

	1	2	3	4	5	
EASY	○	○	○	○	○	HARD

TRAIL TYPE

☐ LOOP   ☐ ONE WAY

☐ OUT & BACK   ☐ OTHERS

GEAR & EQUIPMENT

ANIMALS & PLANTS

ROUTE HIGHLIGHTS

MILESTONE	TIME	NOTE

	TRAIL NAME
	LOCATION
	DATE
	COMPANIONS

	START TIME
	END TIME
	DURATION
	DISTANCE
	ALTITUDE

WEATHER CONDITIONS

		☀	⛅	🌧	⛈	❄
🌡	—	☐	☐	☐	☐	☐
🚩	—					

TERRAIN LEVEL

EASY	1 ○	2 ○	3 ○	4 ○	5 ○	HARD

TRAIL TYPE

☐ LOOP	☐ ONE WAY
☐ OUT & BACK	☐ OTHERS

GEAR & EQUIPMENT

ANIMALS & PLANTS

ROUTE HIGHLIGHTS

MILESTONE	TIME	NOTE

TRAIL NAME

LOCATION

DATE

COMPANIONS

START TIME

END TIME

DURATION

DISTANCE

ALTITUDE

WEATHER CONDITIONS

☀ ⛅ 🌧 ⛈ ❄

☐ ☐ ☐ ☐ ☐

TERRAIN LEVEL

EASY 1 ◯ 2 ◯ 3 ◯ 4 ◯ 5 ◯ HARD

TRAIL TYPE

☐ LOOP   ☐ ONE WAY

☐ OUT & BACK   ☐ OTHERS

GEAR & EQUIPMENT

ANIMALS & PLANTS

ROUTE HIGHLIGHTS

MILESTONE	TIME	NOTE

	TRAIL NAME	
	LOCATION	
	DATE	
	COMPANIONS	

WEATHER CONDITIONS

🌡 ___ ☀ ⛅ 🌧 ⛈ ❄

🚩 ___ ☐ ☐ ☐ ☐ ☐

	START TIME	
	END TIME	
	DURATION	
	DISTANCE	
	ALTITUDE	

TERRAIN LEVEL

EASY ⓵ ○ ② ○ ③ ○ ④ ○ ⑤ ○ HARD
1 2 3 4 5

TRAIL TYPE

☐ LOOP	☐ ONE WAY
☐ OUT & BACK	☐ OTHERS

GEAR & EQUIPMENT

ANIMALS & PLANTS

ROUTE HIGHLIGHTS

🗺 MILESTONE	🕐 TIME	📝 NOTE

TRAIL NAME

LOCATION

DATE

COMPANIONS

START TIME

END TIME

DURATION

DISTANCE

ALTITUDE

WEATHER CONDITIONS

TERRAIN LEVEL

	1	2	3	4	5	
EASY	○	○	○	○	○	HARD

TRAIL TYPE

☐ LOOP	☐ ONE WAY
☐ OUT & BACK	☐ OTHERS

GEAR & EQUIPMENT

ANIMALS & PLANTS

ROUTE HIGHLIGHTS

MILESTONE	TIME	NOTE

TRAIL NAME

LOCATION

DATE

COMPANIONS

START TIME

END TIME

DURATION

DISTANCE

ALTITUDE

WEATHER CONDITIONS

TERRAIN LEVEL

EASY 1 2 3 4 5 HARD

TRAIL TYPE

| ☐ LOOP | ☐ ONE WAY |
| ☐ OUT & BACK | ☐ OTHERS |

GEAR & EQUIPMENT

ANIMALS & PLANTS

ROUTE HIGHLIGHTS

MILESTONE	TIME	NOTE

TRAIL NAME

LOCATION

DATE

COMPANIONS

START TIME

END TIME

DURATION

DISTANCE

ALTITUDE

WEATHER CONDITIONS

temperature —

wind —

☐ ☐ ☐ ☐ ☐

TERRAIN LEVEL

EASY 1 2 3 4 5 HARD
○ ○ ○ ○ ○

TRAIL TYPE

| ☐ LOOP | ☐ ONE WAY |
| ☐ OUT & BACK | ☐ OTHERS |

GEAR & EQUIPMENT

ANIMALS & PLANTS

ROUTE HIGHLIGHTS

MILESTONE	TIME	NOTE

TRAIL NAME

LOCATION

DATE

COMPANIONS

START TIME

END TIME

DURATION

DISTANCE

ALTITUDE

WEATHER CONDITIONS

☀ ⛅ ☁ ⛈ ❄

☐ ☐ ☐ ☐ ☐

TERRAIN LEVEL

EASY 1 2 3 4 5 HARD
○ ○ ○ ○ ○

TRAIL TYPE

| ☐ LOOP | ☐ ONE WAY |
| ☐ OUT & BACK | ☐ OTHERS |

GEAR & EQUIPMENT

ANIMALS & PLANTS

ROUTE HIGHLIGHTS

MILESTONE	TIME	NOTE

TRAIL NAME

LOCATION

DATE

COMPANIONS

START TIME

END TIME

DURATION

DISTANCE

ALTITUDE

WEATHER CONDITIONS

TERRAIN LEVEL

1   2   3   4   5

EASY   HARD

TRAIL TYPE

☐ LOOP   ☐ ONE WAY

☐ OUT & BACK   ☐ OTHERS

GEAR & EQUIPMENT

ANIMALS & PLANTS

ROUTE HIGHLIGHTS

MILESTONE	TIME	NOTE

	TRAIL NAME
	LOCATION
	DATE
	COMPANIONS

	START TIME
	END TIME
	DURATION
	DISTANCE
	ALTITUDE

WEATHER CONDITIONS

☀️ ⛅ 🌧️ ⛈️ ❄️

☐ ☐ ☐ ☐ ☐

TERRAIN LEVEL

EASY	1 ○	2 ○	3 ○	4 ○	5 ○	HARD

TRAIL TYPE

☐ LOOP	☐ ONE WAY
☐ OUT & BACK	☐ OTHERS

GEAR & EQUIPMENT

ANIMALS & PLANTS

ROUTE HIGHLIGHTS

MILESTONE	TIME	NOTE

TRAIL NAME	
LOCATION	
DATE	
COMPANIONS	

WEATHER CONDITIONS

🌡 _____   ☀ ⛅ 🌧 ⛈ ❄

🏳 _____   ☐ ☐ ☐ ☐ ☐

START TIME	
END TIME	
DURATION	
DISTANCE	
ALTITUDE	

TERRAIN LEVEL

EASY 1 ○ 2 ○ 3 ○ 4 ○ 5 ○ HARD

TRAIL TYPE

☐ LOOP	☐ ONE WAY
☐ OUT & BACK	☐ OTHERS

GEAR & EQUIPMENT

ANIMALS & PLANTS

ROUTE HIGHLIGHTS

MILESTONE	TIME	NOTE

TRAIL NAME

LOCATION

DATE

COMPANIONS

START TIME

END TIME

DURATION

DISTANCE

ALTITUDE

WEATHER CONDITIONS

TERRAIN LEVEL

EASY | 1 | 2 | 3 | 4 | 5 | HARD

TRAIL TYPE

| ☐ LOOP | ☐ ONE WAY |
| ☐ OUT & BACK | ☐ OTHERS |

GEAR & EQUIPMENT

ANIMALS & PLANTS

ROUTE HIGHLIGHTS

MILESTONE	TIME	NOTE

TRAIL NAME

LOCATION

DATE

COMPANIONS

START TIME

END TIME

DURATION

DISTANCE

ALTITUDE

WEATHER CONDITIONS

——

——

TERRAIN LEVEL

EASY 1 2 3 4 5 HARD

TRAIL TYPE

- [ ] LOOP
- [ ] ONE WAY
- [ ] OUT & BACK
- [ ] OTHERS

GEAR & EQUIPMENT

ANIMALS & PLANTS

ROUTE HIGHLIGHTS

MILESTONE	TIME	NOTE

TRAIL NAME

LOCATION

DATE

COMPANIONS

START TIME

END TIME

DURATION

DISTANCE

ALTITUDE

WEATHER CONDITIONS

TERRAIN LEVEL

EASY   1   2   3   4   5   HARD

TRAIL TYPE

| ☐ LOOP | ☐ ONE WAY |
| ☐ OUT & BACK | ☐ OTHERS |

GEAR & EQUIPMENT

ANIMALS & PLANTS

ROUTE HIGHLIGHTS

MILESTONE	TIME	NOTE

TRAIL NAME

LOCATION

DATE

COMPANIONS

START TIME

END TIME

DURATION

DISTANCE

ALTITUDE

WEATHER CONDITIONS

TERRAIN LEVEL

	1	2	3	4	5	
EASY	◯	◯	◯	◯	◯	HARD

TRAIL TYPE

☐ LOOP	☐ ONE WAY
☐ OUT & BACK	☐ OTHERS

GEAR & EQUIPMENT

ANIMALS & PLANTS

ROUTE HIGHLIGHTS

MILESTONE	TIME	NOTE

TRAIL NAME

LOCATION

DATE

COMPANIONS

START TIME

END TIME

DURATION

DISTANCE

ALTITUDE

WEATHER CONDITIONS

TERRAIN LEVEL

EASY 1 2 3 4 5 HARD

TRAIL TYPE

| ☐ LOOP | ☐ ONE WAY |
| ☐ OUT & BACK | ☐ OTHERS |

GEAR & EQUIPMENT

ANIMALS & PLANTS

ROUTE HIGHLIGHTS

MILESTONE	TIME	NOTE

TRAIL NAME

LOCATION

DATE

COMPANIONS

START TIME

END TIME

DURATION

DISTANCE

ALTITUDE

WEATHER CONDITIONS

TERRAIN LEVEL

EASY 1 2 3 4 5 HARD

TRAIL TYPE

| ☐ LOOP | ☐ ONE WAY |
| ☐ OUT & BACK | ☐ OTHERS |

GEAR & EQUIPMENT

ANIMALS & PLANTS

ROUTE HIGHLIGHTS

MILESTONE	TIME	NOTE

TRAIL NAME

LOCATION

DATE

COMPANIONS

START TIME

END TIME

DURATION

DISTANCE

ALTITUDE

WEATHER CONDITIONS

🌡 ——   ☀️ ⛅ 🌧 ⛈ ❄️

🚩 ——   ☐   ☐   ☐   ☐   ☐

TERRAIN LEVEL

EASY	1	2	3	4	5	HARD
◯	◯	◯	◯	◯	◯	

TRAIL TYPE

☐ LOOP	☐ ONE WAY
☐ OUT & BACK	☐ OTHERS

GEAR & EQUIPMENT

ANIMALS & PLANTS

ROUTE HIGHLIGHTS

MILESTONE	TIME	NOTE

TRAIL NAME

LOCATION

DATE

COMPANIONS

START TIME

END TIME

DURATION

DISTANCE

ALTITUDE

WEATHER CONDITIONS

TERRAIN LEVEL

EASY 1 2 3 4 5 HARD

TRAIL TYPE

| ☐ LOOP | ☐ ONE WAY |
| ☐ OUT & BACK | ☐ OTHERS |

GEAR & EQUIPMENT

ANIMALS & PLANTS

ROUTE HIGHLIGHTS

MILESTONE	TIME	NOTE

TRAIL NAME

LOCATION

DATE

COMPANIONS

START TIME

END TIME

DURATION

DISTANCE

ALTITUDE

WEATHER CONDITIONS

TERRAIN LEVEL

EASY — 1 — 2 — 3 — 4 — 5 — HARD

TRAIL TYPE

| ☐ LOOP | ☐ ONE WAY |
| ☐ OUT & BACK | ☐ OTHERS |

GEAR & EQUIPMENT

ANIMALS & PLANTS

ROUTE HIGHLIGHTS

MILESTONE	TIME	NOTE

	TRAIL NAME
	LOCATION
	DATE
	COMPANIONS

	START TIME
	END TIME
	DURATION
	DISTANCE
	ALTITUDE

WEATHER CONDITIONS

☀ ⛅ 🌧 ⛈ ❄

☐ ☐ ☐ ☐ ☐

TERRAIN LEVEL

EASY 1 ○ 2 ○ 3 ○ 4 ○ 5 ○ HARD

TRAIL TYPE

☐ LOOP	☐ ONE WAY
☐ OUT & BACK	☐ OTHERS

GEAR & EQUIPMENT

ANIMALS & PLANTS

ROUTE HIGHLIGHTS

MILESTONE	TIME	NOTE

TRAIL NAME

LOCATION

DATE

COMPANIONS

START TIME

END TIME

DURATION

DISTANCE

ALTITUDE

WEATHER CONDITIONS

TERRAIN LEVEL

EASY | 1 | 2 | 3 | 4 | 5 | HARD

TRAIL TYPE

- [ ] LOOP
- [ ] ONE WAY
- [ ] OUT & BACK
- [ ] OTHERS

GEAR & EQUIPMENT

ANIMALS & PLANTS

ROUTE HIGHLIGHTS

MILESTONE	TIME	NOTE

TRAIL NAME

LOCATION

DATE

COMPANIONS

START TIME

END TIME

DURATION

DISTANCE

ALTITUDE

WEATHER CONDITIONS

TERRAIN LEVEL

EASY | 1 | 2 | 3 | 4 | 5 | HARD

TRAIL TYPE

| ☐ LOOP | ☐ ONE WAY |
| ☐ OUT & BACK | ☐ OTHERS |

GEAR & EQUIPMENT

ANIMALS & PLANTS

ROUTE HIGHLIGHTS

MILESTONE	TIME	NOTE

TRAIL NAME

LOCATION

DATE

COMPANIONS

START TIME

END TIME

DURATION

DISTANCE

ALTITUDE

WEATHER CONDITIONS

TERRAIN LEVEL

1   2   3   4   5

EASY   HARD

TRAIL TYPE

| ☐ LOOP | ☐ ONE WAY |
| ☐ OUT & BACK | ☐ OTHERS |

GEAR & EQUIPMENT

ANIMALS & PLANTS

ROUTE HIGHLIGHTS

MILESTONE	TIME	NOTE

TRAIL NAME

LOCATION

DATE

COMPANIONS

START TIME

END TIME

DURATION

DISTANCE

ALTITUDE

WEATHER CONDITIONS

TERRAIN LEVEL

	1	2	3	4	5	
EASY	○	○	○	○	○	HARD

TRAIL TYPE

☐ LOOP	☐ ONE WAY
☐ OUT & BACK	☐ OTHERS

GEAR & EQUIPMENT

ANIMALS & PLANTS

ROUTE HIGHLIGHTS

MILESTONE	TIME	NOTE

TRAIL NAME

LOCATION

DATE

COMPANIONS

START TIME

END TIME

DURATION

DISTANCE

ALTITUDE

WEATHER CONDITIONS

TERRAIN LEVEL

EASY 1 2 3 4 5 HARD

TRAIL TYPE

- [ ] LOOP
- [ ] ONE WAY
- [ ] OUT & BACK
- [ ] OTHERS

GEAR & EQUIPMENT

ANIMALS & PLANTS

ROUTE HIGHLIGHTS

MILESTONE	TIME	NOTE

TRAIL NAME

LOCATION

DATE

COMPANIONS

START TIME

END TIME

DURATION

DISTANCE

ALTITUDE

WEATHER CONDITIONS

TERRAIN LEVEL

	1	2	3	4	5	
EASY	○	○	○	○	○	HARD

TRAIL TYPE

☐ LOOP	☐ ONE WAY
☐ OUT & BACK	☐ OTHERS

GEAR & EQUIPMENT

ANIMALS & PLANTS

ROUTE HIGHLIGHTS

MILESTONE	TIME	NOTE

	TRAIL NAME
	LOCATION
	DATE
	COMPANIONS

	START TIME
	END TIME
	DURATION
	DISTANCE
	ALTITUDE

WEATHER CONDITIONS

	☀️	⛅	🌧️	⛈️	❄️
	☐	☐	☐	☐	☐

TERRAIN LEVEL

EASY ○ 1 ○ 2 ○ 3 ○ 4 ○ 5 HARD

TRAIL TYPE

☐ LOOP	☐ ONE WAY
☐ OUT & BACK	☐ OTHERS

GEAR & EQUIPMENT

ANIMALS & PLANTS

ROUTE HIGHLIGHTS

MILESTONE	TIME	NOTE

TRAIL NAME

LOCATION

DATE

COMPANIONS

START TIME

END TIME

DURATION

DISTANCE

ALTITUDE

WEATHER CONDITIONS

TERRAIN LEVEL

EASY 1 2 3 4 5 HARD

TRAIL TYPE

☐ LOOP   ☐ ONE WAY

☐ OUT & BACK   ☐ OTHERS

GEAR & EQUIPMENT

ANIMALS & PLANTS

ROUTE HIGHLIGHTS

MILESTONE	TIME	NOTE

TRAIL NAME

LOCATION

DATE

COMPANIONS

START TIME

END TIME

DURATION

DISTANCE

ALTITUDE

WEATHER CONDITIONS

TERRAIN LEVEL

EASY 1 2 3 4 5 HARD

TRAIL TYPE

☐ LOOP		☐ ONE WAY
☐ OUT & BACK		☐ OTHERS

GEAR & EQUIPMENT

ANIMALS & PLANTS

ROUTE HIGHLIGHTS

MILESTONE	TIME	NOTE

TRAIL NAME

LOCATION

DATE

COMPANIONS

START TIME

END TIME

DURATION

DISTANCE

ALTITUDE

WEATHER CONDITIONS

TERRAIN LEVEL

EASY 1 2 3 4 5 HARD

TRAIL TYPE

| ☐ LOOP | ☐ ONE WAY |
| ☐ OUT & BACK | ☐ OTHERS |

GEAR & EQUIPMENT

ANIMALS & PLANTS

ROUTE HIGHLIGHTS

MILESTONE	TIME	NOTE

🪧 TRAIL NAME
📍 LOCATION
📅 DATE
👥 COMPANIONS

🥾 START TIME
🚩 END TIME
⏱️ DURATION
📍 DISTANCE
⛰️ ALTITUDE

WEATHER CONDITIONS

🌡️ ___ ☀️ ⛅ 🌧️ ⛈️ ❄️

🚩 ___ ☐ ☐ ☐ ☐ ☐

TERRAIN LEVEL

EASY ○ 1 ○ 2 ○ 3 ○ 4 ○ 5 HARD

TRAIL TYPE

☐ LOOP	☐ ONE WAY
☐ OUT & BACK	☐ OTHERS

GEAR & EQUIPMENT

ANIMALS & PLANTS

ROUTE HIGHLIGHTS

🗺️ MILESTONE	🕐 TIME	📝 NOTE

	TRAIL NAME
	LOCATION
	DATE
	COMPANIONS

	START TIME
	END TIME
	DURATION
	DISTANCE
	ALTITUDE

WEATHER CONDITIONS

TERRAIN LEVEL

EASY 1 2 3 4 5 HARD

TRAIL TYPE

☐ LOOP	☐ ONE WAY
☐ OUT & BACK	☐ OTHERS

GEAR & EQUIPMENT

ANIMALS & PLANTS

ROUTE HIGHLIGHTS

MILESTONE	TIME	NOTE

TRAIL NAME

LOCATION

DATE

COMPANIONS

START TIME

END TIME

DURATION

DISTANCE

ALTITUDE

WEATHER CONDITIONS

TERRAIN LEVEL

EASY 1 2 3 4 5 HARD

TRAIL TYPE

| ☐ LOOP | ☐ ONE WAY |
| ☐ OUT & BACK | ☐ OTHERS |

GEAR & EQUIPMENT

ANIMALS & PLANTS

ROUTE HIGHLIGHTS

MILESTONE	TIME	NOTE

TRAIL NAME		WEATHER CONDITIONS

TRAIL NAME
LOCATION
DATE
COMPANIONS

WEATHER CONDITIONS

START TIME
END TIME
DURATION
DISTANCE
ALTITUDE

TERRAIN LEVEL

EASY	1	2	3	4	5	HARD

TRAIL TYPE

☐ LOOP	☐ ONE WAY
☐ OUT & BACK	☐ OTHERS

GEAR & EQUIPMENT

ANIMALS & PLANTS

ROUTE HIGHLIGHTS

MILESTONE	TIME	NOTE

TRAIL NAME

LOCATION

DATE

COMPANIONS

START TIME

END TIME

DURATION

DISTANCE

ALTITUDE

WEATHER CONDITIONS

☀️ ⛅ 🌧️ ⛈️ ❄️

☐ ☐ ☐ ☐ ☐

TERRAIN LEVEL

EASY	1	2	3	4	5	HARD

TRAIL TYPE

☐ LOOP	☐ ONE WAY
☐ OUT & BACK	☐ OTHERS

GEAR & EQUIPMENT

ANIMALS & PLANTS

ROUTE HIGHLIGHTS

MILESTONE	TIME	NOTE

TRAIL NAME

LOCATION

DATE

COMPANIONS

START TIME

END TIME

DURATION

DISTANCE

ALTITUDE

WEATHER CONDITIONS

TERRAIN LEVEL

EASY 1 2 3 4 5 HARD

TRAIL TYPE

| ☐ LOOP | ☐ ONE WAY |
| ☐ OUT & BACK | ☐ OTHERS |

GEAR & EQUIPMENT

ANIMALS & PLANTS

ROUTE HIGHLIGHTS

MILESTONE	TIME	NOTE

TRAIL NAME

LOCATION

DATE

COMPANIONS

START TIME

END TIME

DURATION

DISTANCE

ALTITUDE

WEATHER CONDITIONS

TERRAIN LEVEL

EASY 1   2   3   4   5 HARD

TRAIL TYPE

| ☐ LOOP | ☐ ONE WAY |
| ☐ OUT & BACK | ☐ OTHERS |

GEAR & EQUIPMENT

ANIMALS & PLANTS

ROUTE HIGHLIGHTS

MILESTONE	TIME	NOTE

| TRAIL NAME |
| LOCATION |
| DATE |
| COMPANIONS |

WEATHER CONDITIONS

☀ ⛅ ☁ 🌧 ❄

☐ ☐ ☐ ☐ ☐

| START TIME |
| END TIME |
| DURATION |
| DISTANCE |
| ALTITUDE |

TERRAIN LEVEL

EASY 1 2 3 4 5 HARD
○ ○ ○ ○ ○

TRAIL TYPE

| ☐ LOOP | ☐ ONE WAY |
| ☐ OUT & BACK | ☐ OTHERS |

GEAR & EQUIPMENT

ANIMALS & PLANTS

ROUTE HIGHLIGHTS

MILESTONE	TIME	NOTE

TRAIL NAME

LOCATION

DATE

COMPANIONS

START TIME

END TIME

DURATION

DISTANCE

ALTITUDE

WEATHER CONDITIONS

TERRAIN LEVEL

| | 1 | 2 | 3 | 4 | 5 | |
EASY ○ ○ ○ ○ ○ HARD

TRAIL TYPE

| ☐ LOOP | ☐ ONE WAY |
| ☐ OUT & BACK | ☐ OTHERS |

GEAR & EQUIPMENT

ANIMALS & PLANTS

ROUTE HIGHLIGHTS

MILESTONE	TIME	NOTE

TRAIL NAME

LOCATION

DATE

COMPANIONS

START TIME

END TIME

DURATION

DISTANCE

ALTITUDE

WEATHER CONDITIONS

TERRAIN LEVEL

EASY 1 2 3 4 5 HARD

TRAIL TYPE

| ☐ LOOP | ☐ ONE WAY |
| ☐ OUT & BACK | ☐ OTHERS |

GEAR & EQUIPMENT

ANIMALS & PLANTS

ROUTE HIGHLIGHTS

MILESTONE	TIME	NOTE

TRAIL NAME	WEATHER CONDITIONS

TRAIL NAME

LOCATION

DATE

COMPANIONS

WEATHER CONDITIONS

Temperature: ___ ☀ ⛅ 🌧 ⛈ ❄

Wind: ___ ☐ ☐ ☐ ☐ ☐

START TIME

END TIME

DURATION

DISTANCE

ALTITUDE

TERRAIN LEVEL

EASY 1 2 3 4 5 HARD
○ ○ ○ ○ ○

TRAIL TYPE

☐ LOOP   ☐ ONE WAY

☐ OUT & BACK   ☐ OTHERS

GEAR & EQUIPMENT

ANIMALS & PLANTS

ROUTE HIGHLIGHTS

🗺 MILESTONE	🕐 TIME	📝 NOTE

TRAIL NAME

LOCATION

DATE

COMPANIONS

START TIME

END TIME

DURATION

DISTANCE

ALTITUDE

WEATHER CONDITIONS

TERRAIN LEVEL

EASY ○ 1 ○ 2 ○ 3 ○ 4 ○ 5 HARD

TRAIL TYPE

| LOOP | ONE WAY |
| OUT & BACK | OTHERS |

GEAR & EQUIPMENT

ANIMALS & PLANTS

ROUTE HIGHLIGHTS

MILESTONE	TIME	NOTE

TRAIL NAME

LOCATION

DATE

COMPANIONS

START TIME

END TIME

DURATION

DISTANCE

ALTITUDE

WEATHER CONDITIONS

🌡 —   ☀ ⛅ 🌧 ⛈ ❄

🎏 —   ☐ ☐ ☐ ☐ ☐

TERRAIN LEVEL

EASY ○ 1 2 3 4 5 HARD

TRAIL TYPE

| ☐ LOOP | ☐ ONE WAY |
| ☐ OUT & BACK | ☐ OTHERS |

GEAR & EQUIPMENT

ANIMALS & PLANTS

ROUTE HIGHLIGHTS

MILESTONE	TIME	NOTE

TRAIL NAME

LOCATION

DATE

COMPANIONS

START TIME

END TIME

DURATION

DISTANCE

ALTITUDE

WEATHER CONDITIONS

TERRAIN LEVEL

EASY 1 2 3 4 5 HARD

TRAIL TYPE

☐ LOOP   ☐ ONE WAY

☐ OUT & BACK   ☐ OTHERS

GEAR & EQUIPMENT

ANIMALS & PLANTS

ROUTE HIGHLIGHTS

MILESTONE	TIME	NOTE

TRAIL NAME

LOCATION

DATE

COMPANIONS

START TIME

END TIME

DURATION

DISTANCE

ALTITUDE

WEATHER CONDITIONS

TERRAIN LEVEL

EASY 1 2 3 4 5 HARD

TRAIL TYPE

☐ LOOP ☐ ONE WAY

☐ OUT & BACK ☐ OTHERS

GEAR & EQUIPMENT

ANIMALS & PLANTS

ROUTE HIGHLIGHTS

MILESTONE	TIME	NOTE

TRAIL NAME

LOCATION

DATE

COMPANIONS

START TIME

END TIME

DURATION

DISTANCE

ALTITUDE

WEATHER CONDITIONS

TERRAIN LEVEL

| EASY | 1 | 2 | 3 | 4 | 5 | HARD |

TRAIL TYPE

| ☐ LOOP | ☐ ONE WAY |
| ☐ OUT & BACK | ☐ OTHERS |

GEAR & EQUIPMENT

ANIMALS & PLANTS

ROUTE HIGHLIGHTS

MILESTONE	TIME	NOTE

Printed in Great Britain
by Amazon

86156353R00071